Deliciously VEGAN EVERYDAY Kitchen

FUSS-FREE. GLUTEN-FREE. PLANT-POWERED RECIPES

SIBEL HODGE

Deliciously Vegan Everyday Kitchen
Sibel Hodge

Copyright © Sibel Hodge 2020

The moral right of the author has been asserted. All rights reserved in all media. No part of this book may be reproduced or transmitted in any form by any means, electronic or mechanical (including but not limited to: the Internet, photocopying, recording or by any information storage and retrieval system), without prior permission in writing from the author and/or publisher.

The author acknowledges the trademarked status and trademark owners of various products referenced in this work, which have been used without permission. The publication/use of these trademarks is not authorized, associated with, or sponsored by the trademark owners.

Disclaimer: This book is not intended as health/dietary advice, and it does not replace any medical/health advice given to you by your doctor. All labels and packaging should be checked thoroughly by the reader to ensure they are using a gluten-free/vegan product. The author and publisher disclaim all liability in connection with the use of this book.

Contents

introduction v
Quick Tips vii

MEZE & DIPS 1
Hummus 1
Guacamole 2
Tortilla Chips 2
Vegan "Egg" Mayonnaise 3
Easy Peasy Spinach Pesto 4
Vegan Feta Dip 4
Bbq Dip 5
Ranch-Style Mayonnaise 5
Smoky Chickpea Mash 6
Olives With Garlic And Lemon 6
Yoghurt And Cucumber Dip 7
Lemon Tahini Dip 8
Tomato And Chilli Dip 8

SUMPTUOUS SALADS 9
Beetroot Salad 9
Chickpea Salad 10
Spiced Bean Salad 10
Greek Salad 11
Turkish Potato Salad 12
Onion Salad 12
Rocket Salad 13
Green Salad With Walnuts And Figs 13
Couscous Salad 14
Quick Bean Salad 15
Spicy Pepper Salad 15

SIDES & SUNDRIES 16
Indian Mushroom Rice 16
Middle Eastern Potatoes 16
Vegetable Pilaf 17

Cheesy Potato Bake 18
Bbq Mushrooms 18
Vermicelli Rice 19
Sexy Cabbage 20
Herby Potato Wedges 20
Caramelised Roast Vegetables 21
Coriander Carrots 22
Mediterranean Green Beans 23
Minted Potatoes 23
Fried Aubergine With Tomato Salsa 24
Maple Sprouts 25
Golden Turmeric Rice 25
Potato Cakes 26
Quick Parmesan 27
Onion Gravy 27

LIGHT BITES & MAIN MEALS 28
Cauliflower Mincemeat 28
Mango And Sweet Potato Masala 28
Basil Pesto Pasta 29
Southern Fried Tofu Nuggets 30
Moussaka 31
Spanish Frittata 32
Turkish Casserole 33
Onion Bhajis With Tomato Chutney 34
Salt-And-Pepper Tofu 35
Rich Spaghetti Bolognese 36
Cannellini Bean Fritters 36
Asparagus And Mushroom Risotto 37
Scrambled "Eggy" Tofu 38
Greek-Style Shepherd's Pie 39
Turkish Pizza 40
Easy Lasagne 41
Cauliflower And Broccoli Cheese 42
No-Fuss Paella 43
Sticky Bbq Tofu 44
Speedy Asian Noodles 45
Chilli Con Carne 46

Quick Pita Pizza 47
Simple Garlic Pasta 48
Aubergine Parmigiana 49
Sweet And Sour Tofu 50
Moroccan Cauliflower Steaks 51
Lentil And Chestnut Goulash 52
Braised Mince Bourguignonne 53
Potato-Crust Pizza 54
Oven-Baked Pasta 55
Shepherd's Pie 56
Baked Orange Tofu 57
Spicy Buffalo Cauliflower Bites 58
Chinese Curry 59
Sicilian Aubergine Pasta 60
Turkish Bean Stew 61
Stuffed Peppers 62
Kung Pao Tofu 63
Creamy Stroganoff 64
Marinades 65

About the Author 66
Also by Sibel Hodge 67

INTRODUCTION

A big hello and welcome to my second vegan cookbook. Whether you're a new vegan, or you're dabbling in plant-based foods and are looking for exciting alternatives to your diet, or you already don't use animal products at all, this book is for everyone wanting to explore a vegan diet. Inside you'll find over eighty everyday recipes that are healthy, low fat, low in cholesterol, and packed full of nutritious plant power. The beauty of this cookbook is that the recipes are quick, fuss-free, and easily made gluten-free (gluten-free markers are added in the recipe where needed in brackets).

Even going back a few years ago a lot of people thought all vegans ate were salad, nuts, and chips, with the odd bit of grass thrown in there. But cooking plant-based food has given me a whole new range of possibilities, ideas, tastes, and much more creativity in the kitchen. I've eaten a more varied diet since being vegan than I ever did before, and hopefully my recipes will show you that cooking delicious, plant-based foods has never been so easy. Maybe it will open up your eyes to a whole range of ingredients you've never explored. Or inspire you to experiment with existing produce that often get a bad reputation for being boring or bland. I'll take you on a culinary trip from the Mediterranean to Asia, India, and around the world, and I hope you enjoy the dishes as much as I do.

These recipes should be used as a guideline because you know your taste buds better than anyone else does. If you want to substitute one veg or spice for another that you like more, then go for it. This is how great recipes are created, and it's all about making the food work for you. If you like the dishes in here then please check out my first vegan cookbook, *Deliciously Vegan Soup Kitchen*.

For those who don't know my story, let me tell you a little bit about how this book was born. Usually, you can find me writing novels, especially thrillers, but I also have a special passion for food and have been cooking since I was about ten years old, under the watchful eye of my nan, who was a fabulous chef. But even though I usually kill my characters off for a living, don't panic! The recipes in this book won't be bumping anyone off. In contrast, as a qualified health and fitness professional with a special interest in nutrition, I can say wholeheartedly that the health benefits of a vegan diet are impressive and wide-ranging.

My journey to veganism stemmed from my love of animals. I've always been a compassionate and empathetic person, but being a meat eater for most of my life, I'd never made the connection that what I ate and my core beliefs were at polar opposites to each other. I became vegetarian and then started looking into veganism more when I realised that although I'd stopped eating meat, the dairy, egg, fishing, and every other animal agricultural industry that exploited our fellow sentient beings was equally, if not more so, horrific and tortuous. I watched the documentary *Earthlings* – actually, I *forced* myself to watch it, because it's very graphic – but I'd realised by then that every choice I made in life affected someone or something else. And my dietary choices and what I consumed had a direct and significant effect on the animals that I loved. Five minutes into the documentary I turned vegan, which was five years ago now, and I haven't looked back since. But I do a lot of research for my novels, and that research didn't stop with just my work. The more I explored information about veganism the more I realised the amazingly positive health benefits it has and the exponentially damaging environmental effect animal agriculture has on the only home we have – planet earth.

But enough about me. The most important thing with cooking is to have fun with it, so let's get cracking on with the good bit...food!

Sibel XX

QUICK TIPS

TOFU

Don't be scared of tofu! It's amazingly versatile, and because I'm using it in several of the following recipes, I'm including some quick info for you here.

It comes in many varieties: firm, extra-firm, soft, and silken. Basically, the difference is in how much water is pressed out of the tofu. For the forthcoming recipes I'm using firm tofu, which maintains its shape and texture and is great for dishes that call for meaty-like chunks. I also use extra-firm silken tofu, which is more jelly-like and perfect for sauces, scrambles, and soups. Wherever possible choose non-GMO, organic tofu.

The first thing you need to do when cooking with tofu is to press it. If you don't have a tofu press, the next best thing is easy peasy. Simply drain the tofu and pat it in between a tea towel or some kitchen paper. Then place it between two plates and put a weight on top. I use a can of tomatoes or beans. This helps to press out all the excess water it's packed in. After about half an hour you're good to go with it.

OLIVE OIL

Being from a Mediterranean family, I use olive oil a *lot*! But not all olive oil is created equal. Where possible, try to use good quality, extra-virgin olive oil. The extra-virgin variety is made from pure, cold-pressed olives, whereas regular olive oil will be made with a blend of cold-pressed and processed oils. The more processed variety will give you a lighter-coloured, more neutral-flavoured oil. But the olive oil gold standard of extra-virgin will have a wholesome and deliciously rich flavour to it.

FRESH GINGER

I buy big chunks of fresh root ginger and cut them into 1 inch pieces, which I store in the freezer (they keep for months). It's much easier to grate into dishes after they've been removed from the freezer for a couple of minutes and then peeled.

GRATING TOMATOES

For speed, some of the tomato-based recipes use canned tomatoes, but creating your own grated tomatoes for sauces using fresh produce is quick and easy. Just hold the stem end and slice off the other end. Then coarsely grate on a regular cheese grater into a bowl. The flesh and juice will come away easily and end up in the bowl, and the flesh will be left in your hand.

CHICKPEA (GRAM) FLOUR

As the name suggests, chickpea flour is made from dry, ground chickpeas (also known as garbanzo beans). I use it a lot, because it's gluten-free and is great for creating batters or thickening up dishes and has a creamy, nutty taste. I use a traditional Indian variety, but it's readily available in most supermarkets these days.

SALT

People have used salt as a seasoning for thousands of years, and it's eaten on a daily basis around the world. But in the refining process, regular table salt is processed and mixed with anticaking agents and other additives, and I believe Himalayan rock salt is a tastier, healthier alternative. It's naturally pink and unrefined and incorporates many more minerals and trace elements.

NUTRITIONAL YEAST

Nutritional yeast, or, as it's lovingly known, nooch, is a common addition used in vegan cooking. It's deactivated yeast, which means that the yeast cells are killed off during the processing and are inactive in the final product. It's sold in flakes, and the amazing thing about it is that it has a cheesy and nutty flavour all rolled in to one. It's full of minerals, fibre, and vitamins, especially B12.

KALA NAMAK

Kala namak is commonly known as black Himalayan salt, although it's actually a dusty pinkish colour. It has a great sulphur tang to it that tastes very eggy and can transform any vegan egg dish into something truly amazing. Wherever possible, choose unrefined, additive-free kala namak. If you can't find it at your supermarket, you can buy it from health food shops or online.

MEZE & DIPS

HUMMUS

Hummus is a firm favourite meze for all occasions. But the simple dish is giving you a two-for-one special – a delicious dip *and* a great source of dietary fibre and protein. Plus, chickpeas are also low in fat, which is always a bonus. One of the main ingredients is tahini, made from roasted and ground sesame seeds, which can also be used as a dip on its own, mixed with olive oil and garlic. This recipe will take around 10 minutes to make, so it's perfect if you're short of time and need a hummus fix.

400g can of chickpeas – drained and rinsed
Juice of 1 lemon
3 garlic cloves – crushed and chopped
1 tbsp of olive oil
2 tbsp of water
3 tbsp of tahini
1 tsp of sumac **optional*
1 tsp of ground cumin
2 tbsp of chopped flat-leaf parsley
1 tbsp of paprika
½ tsp of chilli flakes **optional*
Salt and pepper to taste

Garnish
Drizzle of olive oil
Dusting of cayenne pepper
Flat-leaf parsley – chopped

1. Put all the ingredients into a food processor and blend until it's a smooth paste.

Serves 2-4

GUACAMOLE

This rich little taste of Mexico in a bowl goes perfectly with my tortilla chip recipe (see next page). I like my guacamole in a rustic, chunky style, but you can always blend the ingredients in to a smoother dip if you prefer.

Tip: For an easy way to prepare avocadoes, cut them in half, rotating around the seed, and separate. Then scoop out the avocado flesh with a spoon into a bowl.

2 avocadoes – peeled and mashed with a fork
¼ of a red onion – diced finely
1 garlic clove – crushed and chopped
Juice of half a lime or lemon
1 large tomato – peeled and diced
½ a green chilli – deseeded and diced finely
1½ tbsp of fresh coriander – chopped
Salt and pepper to taste

1. Add all the ingredients into a bowl and mix well.

Serves 2

TORTILLA CHIPS

It's so easy to make fresh tortilla chips, and baking them gives you a healthier alternative to the deep-fried variety. This recipe gives you crispy, golden chips in no time.

Tip: If you want a flavoured batch, sprinkle over some paprika or smoked paprika or ground cumin before cooking.

continued...

Tortilla Chips continued...

2 (gluten-free/vegan) tortillas - each cut into 8 chip-size triangles.
Salt to taste
Olive oil

1. Place the tortilla chips on a baking tray, evenly spaced out in a single layer (you may need to cook them on two trays). Brush with a little olive oil and sprinkle with salt.
2. Bake in a preheated oven at 180°C for 5 minutes. Turn the chips over with a pair of tongs and bake for another 5 to 8 minutes or until golden and crispy.

Serves 2-4

VEGAN "EGG" MAYONNAISE

One of the things I really missed after being vegan was egg mayo, and this recipe has a real eggy taste and is whipped up in just a few minutes. Full of plant protein, it's perfect as a dip or in a sandwich.

350g (approx 2 cups) of extra-firm silken tofu - crumbled with a fork
1 tsp of vegan Dijon mustard
½ tsp of garlic powder
3 tbsp of vegan mayonnaise
1 tbsp of nutritional yeast *optional*
¼ tsp of kala namak (see Quick Tips)
1 tbsp of flat-leaf parsley - chopped
Salt and black pepper to taste

1. Add all the ingredients into a bowl and mix well.

Serves 1-2

EASY PEASY SPINACH PESTO

Traditionally, pesto was made with a mixture of pine nuts, basil, parmesan, and olive oil, but there are so many great variations you can use. If you want to swap the cashews I'm using for walnuts, pine nuts, or almonds, bring it on. What's good about this recipe is that it tastes great as a dip in its own right but is also amazing on pizza, pasta, in wraps or sandwiches, or as an accompaniment to other main dishes.

75g (approx ½ cup) of raw cashew nuts
2 garlic cloves - peeled
60g (approx 2 cups) of baby spinach
Juice of half a lemon
3 tbsp of nutritional yeast
6 tbsp of olive oil
Salt and pepper to taste

1. Add all ingredients to a food processor and blend into a coarse paste.

Serves 2-4

VEGAN FETA DIP

This takes 5 minutes to prepare and is great with warm (gluten-free) pita bread or with fresh raw veggies. You can use any vegan feta-style or soft cheese.

200 g (approx 1½ cups) of vegan feta or other vegan soft cheese
Juice of half a lemon
1 tsp of dried mint
1 garlic clove - crushed and chopped
1-2 tbsp of olive oil

Garnish
Paprika

1. Mash the ingredients together and serve.

Serves 2-4

BBQ DIP

It only takes a handful of ingredients to give you a smoky sweetness mixed with a tangy hit. Use it as a dip or as an accompaniment to other dishes, or brush it over tofu before baking it.

200g of passata
1 tsp of maple syrup
¼ tsp of vegan Dijon mustard
½ tsp of garlic powder
¼ tsp of (gluten-free/vegan) balsamic vinegar
¼ tsp of smoked paprika
1 tsp of (gluten-free) soya sauce or tamari

1. Mix the ingredients in a bowl and serve.

Serves 2-4

RANCH-STYLE MAYONNAISE

When I first went vegan I couldn't find good vegan mayo anywhere and resorted to making my own. But these days it's mayo heaven in supermarkets, and they taste damn good! This recipe gives you a little American-style hit in a bowl.

200g (approx 1 cup) of vegan mayonnaise
½ tsp of garlic powder
½ a spring onion - sliced
1 tbsp of flat-leaf parsley - chopped
½ tsp of chives
1 tsp of lemon juice

1. Add all the ingredients into a bowl and mix well.

Serves 2

SMOKY CHICKPEA MASH

With an infusion of Mexican and Mediterranean flavours, this creamy, smoky dish is a rustic meze delight. If you want to blend it into a smoother dip using a food processor and a little extra water go right ahead.

400g can of chickpeas - drained and rinsed
1 spring onion - sliced
Juice of one lemon
½ tsp of chipotle chilli flakes
½ tsp of smoked paprika
2 tbsp of soya milk
1 tbsp of olive oil
4 tbsp of tahini
1 tsp of vegan Dijon mustard
1½ tsp of garlic powder
1 tbsp of nutritional yeast
Salt and pepper to taste

Garnish
Sliced spring onion

1. Mash the chickpeas with a potato masher then add the rest of the ingredients and mix thoroughly.

Serves 2-4

OLIVES WITH GARLIC AND LEMON

Olives are definitely an acquired taste, and it took me thirty-five years to understand the olive obsession. This famous Cypriot way of preparing green olives turned me from an olive hater into a firm fan. The tangy combo is an amazing mix of zesty, salty, and fragrant delight.

Variation: Use black olives and replace the coriander with chilli flakes and sumac and omit the lemon.

continued...

Olives With Garlic And Lemon continued...

200g (approx 1 cup) of green olives
1 tsp of coriander seeds
1 tbsp of olive oil
1 garlic clove – chopped
Two slices of lemon – cut into small squares

1. Mix together well.
2. Enjoy as a meze or with a cocktail!

Serves 2-4

YOGHURT AND CUCUMBER DIP

Known as tzatziki or cacık, this is a much-eaten dish in South Eastern Europe and the Middle East. It's authentic and completely moreish, and I eat it straight from the bowl with a spoon.

Cucumbers are one of the oldest cultivated vegetables, thought to originate from India. They're very low in calories and actually have fat-burning qualities (yay!). Because of their high water content they're good for eliminating toxins while keeping you hydrated, and their liquid is more beneficial than regular water because it contains many vitamins and minerals. So ten stars for cucumbers!

500g (approx 2 cups) of soya yoghurt (or other vegan yoghurt)
2 garlic cloves – crushed and chopped
½ a cucumber – peeled and diced into small pieces
2 tsp of dried mint
Juice of half a lemon
1 tbsp of olive oil
Salt and pepper to taste

Garnish
Dusting of cayenne pepper *optional*

1. Mix all ingredients together in a bowl.

Serves 2

LEMON TAHINI DIP

Tahini is so versatile. It's rich, creamy, and high in protein. And with just three ingredients, you'll have a deliciously tangy dip with no effort at all.

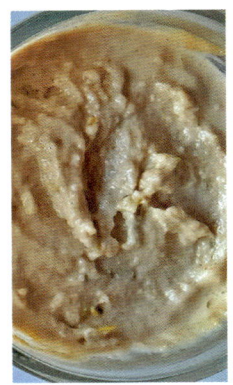

6 tbsp of tahini
Juice and zest of 1 lemon
4 tbsp of water

1. Mix the ingredients in a bowl and serve as a dip or side dish.

Serves 2

TOMATO AND CHILLI DIP

The amount of spiciness in this dip is going to be all down to your personal heatometer. I've tasted some that is hot enough to make you spontaneously combust and some that has a subtle kick but is infused with immense flavour. You can add fresh chillies, chilli paste, or chilli flakes/powder to make it more spicy.

300g of passata
1 spring onion - sliced thinly
1 or 2 chilli peppers - deseeded and chopped finely
1 red pepper - chopped finely
½ tbsp of olive oil
1 garlic clove - chopped
1 tbsp of flat-leaf parsley - chopped
Salt and pepper to taste

1. Add all the ingredients into a bowl and mix well.

A little goes a long way!

SUMPTUOUS SALADS

BEETROOT SALAD

I love this yummy, quick salad. It has a wonderfully earthy taste of beetroot mixed with the sweet and sour balsamic vinegar and garlic. It also looks vibrant and colourful, too, and tastes great garnished with fresh mint. But that's not all...beetroot is often called a superfood and is associated with numerous health benefits, including boosting immunity and lowering cholesterol.

Tip: Wear gloves when peeling cooked beetroot to avoid stained fingers!

4 beetroots - scrubbed with the ends trimmed
3 garlic cloves - chopped
1 tbsp of (gluten-free/vegan) balsamic vinegar
3 tbsp of olive oil
Salt and pepper to taste

1. Put the beetroot in a saucepan and cover with boiling water then simmer for about 30 minutes until tender. To test if they're done, pierce with a knife or skewer. If it slips through the centre easily, you're all set.
2. Remove from the water and allow the beets to cool, then peel away the skin. Be careful, as this is pretty messy! Dice them and place in a bowl with the garlic.
3. Mix the vinegar, olive oil, and salt and pepper and pour over the beetroot. Toss well.

Serves 2-4

CHICKPEA SALAD

This simple Mediterranean salad turns chickpeas (also known as garbanzo beans) into something truly exciting and satisfyingly filling.

400g can of chickpeas - drained and rinsed
½ a red onion - diced
½ a red pepper - diced
100g (approx ¼ cup) of vegan feta (or any vegan cheese) - diced *optional*
Handful of black olives
1 tbsp of olive oil
1 tsp of lemon juice
¼ tsp of ground cumin
2 tbsp of fresh coriander (or any fresh herb) - chopped
Salt and pepper to taste

Garnish
Fresh coriander - chopped

1. Mix ingredients in a salad bowl and toss together well.

Serves 1-2

SPICED BEAN SALAD

This is a quick and healthy dish that's packed full of flavour and has a nice kick from the chilli. I'm using white beans for this recipe, which are great for helping to regulate fat stores in the body by producing alpha-amylase inhibitors. They're a rich source of slow-digesting carbohydrates and rate low on the glycaemic index, so they help to maintain a steady energy level while keeping food cravings away.

continued...

Spiced Bean Salad continued...

400g can of beans (haricot/butter beans/cannellini) – drained and rinsed
½ a red onion – diced
1 green chilli – diced
½ a red pepper – diced
¼ tsp of ground cumin
1 tsp of tomato puree
1 tsp of fresh lemon juice
1 garlic clove – crushed and chopped
1 tbsp of olive oil
Salt and pepper to taste
Olive oil for frying

Garnish
Fresh coriander – chopped

1. Place the beans in a bowl.
2. Fry the onion, fresh chilli, and pepper in olive oil for 5 minutes until soft. Add them to the beans along with the rest of the ingredients.
3. Mix well and serve.

Serves 1-2

GREEK SALAD

Who hasn't heard of Greek salad? This traditional dish has been eaten in Greece and the Mediterranean for years and still hasn't lost its popularity. I'm not surprised, either, because it's easy to make, delicious, and great for eating in hot weather. It tastes fab as a light lunch or accompaniment to a main dish. Feel free to top with olives.

2 tomatoes – diced
½ a red onion – sliced
75g (approx 1 cup) of lettuce – sliced
75g (approx ¾ cup) of cabbage – sliced
A handful of rocket (arugula) – chopped
½ a green pepper – sliced
½ a cucumber – diced
1 tsp of dried oregano
65g (approx ½ cup) of vegan feta cheese
1 tsp of lemon juice
1 tbsp of olive oil
Salt and pepper to taste

1. Place the veggies in a bowl then add the olive oil, lemon juice, oregano, and salt and pepper and mix well. Top with the cheese and serve with (gluten-free) olive bread.

Serves 1-2

TURKISH POTATO SALAD

When you think of potato salad you might picture the variety made with lashings of mayo. But this recipe is as far away from that as you can get. With just a few ingredients you can pump up your potatoes into this scrummy, authentic alternative.

2 medium-sized potatoes - cut into small chunks
1 large spring onion - sliced finely
1 tsp of paprika
½ tsp of sumac *optional*
½ tsp of chilli flakes
3 tbsp of flat-leaf parsley - chopped
4 tbsp of olive oil
½ tsp of garlic powder
Salt and pepper to taste

1. Add the potatoes to a pan of boiling water and simmer for 15 to 20 minutes until cooked. Drain and set aside to allow them to cool.
2. Mix the rest of the ingredients together in a bowl. Add the cooled potatoes and toss well.

Serves 2-4

ONION SALAD

This is a simple salad that's perfect as an accompaniment. Sumac is a Middle Eastern spice and comes from a red berry, which is dried and crushed. It has a tangy, lemony taste that will make the onions zing.

1 onion - sliced
2 tbsp of flat-leaf parsley - chopped
1 tsp of sumac
Salt to taste

1. Mix together well and serve.

Serves 1-2

ROCKET SALAD

It's funny how your tastes change as you get older, isn't it? I used to hate rocket (also called arugula), but I absolutely adore it now and eat it pretty much every day. Rocket gives this salad a wonderfully rich and peppery flavour, and the juices left in the bowl are perfect for mopping up with a chunk of (gluten-free) bread.

25g (approx 1 cup) of baby rocket
75g (approx 1 cup) of lettuce - sliced
75g (approx ¾ cup) of white cabbage - sliced
75g (approx ¾ cup) of red cabbage - sliced
½ a cucumber - diced
1 tomato - peeled and diced
1 tsp of lemon juice
1 tbsp of olive oil
Salt and pepper to taste

1. Place all the ingredients in a salad bowl and mix.

Serves 1-2

GREEN SALAD WITH WALNUTS AND FIGS

Figs and walnuts are a match made in heaven. Because raw figs aren't as sweet as the dried variety, their light flavour and beautiful colour make them perfect for salads. They're also rich in fibre, so be careful about eating too many!

continued...

Green Salad With Walnuts And Figs continued...

Mixture of salad greens: rocket, lettuce, parsley, baby spinach, etc.
2 figs - peeled and quartered
65g (approx ½ cup) of walnuts - chopped and lightly toasted in a pan
Vegan parmesan cheese (or any vegan cheese) - in shavings
2 tbsp of olive oil
1 tbsp of maple syrup
1 tsp of (gluten-free/vegan) balsamic vinegar
Salt and pepper to taste

1. Chop the greens and arrange in a bowl.
2. Add the figs, walnuts, and shavings of cheese on top.
3. Mix the maple syrup, oil, vinegar, and salt and pepper and drizzle over the salad.

Serves 1-2

COUSCOUS SALAD

Couscous is so simple to make and doesn't even require cooking. Just steam and go! Once you have the basic couscous recipe you can then add anything you fancy to make it into an amazing Middle Eastern-style salad or accompaniment. It's also a great alternative to rice. You can get a gluten-free variety now made with corn, but if you're following a gluten-free diet and can't find that then use buckwheat or any kind of as rice a replacement.

150g (approx 1 cup) of (gluten-free) couscous
1 spring onion - sliced
½ a red pepper - diced
½ a green pepper - diced
1 tbsp of lemon juice
½ tsp of chilli flakes
1 garlic clove - crushed and chopped
¾ pint (approx 1½ cups) of boiling water mixed with a (gluten-free) vegetable stock cube
2 tsp of paprika
½ tsp of tomato puree
2 tbsp of olive oil
2 tbsp of flat-leaf parsley - chopped
Salt and pepper to taste

1. Add the couscous to a bowl then pour over the water/stock mix. Cover with a plate and leave to steam for 5 minutes.
2. Fluff up the couscous with a fork then add the rest of the ingredients and stir well. Serve hot or cold with a dollop of vegan yoghurt.

Serves 2

QUICK BEAN SALAD

In just 5 minutes you can transform the humble bean into something fresh, tangy, and packed full of plant protein.

400g can of black-eyed beans - drained and rinsed
Juice of half a lemon
2 tbsp of olive oil
1 tbsp of fresh flat-leaf parsley - chopped
½ tsp of garlic powder

1. Add all the ingredients into a bowl. Mix well and serve.

Serves 1-2

SPICY PEPPER SALAD

This is a traditionally simple Turkish salad that uses cubanelle peppers, which are sweeter in taste, so you get a lush combo of crunchy sweet and spicy flavours. You can also use banana peppers or regular bell peppers. And, of course, you can make this as mild or hot as you like. If you want factor blow-your-head-off on the spicy scale, add more chillies.

2 large tomatoes - peeled and diced
1 or 2 green chillies - deseeded and diced finely
2 green cubanelle peppers - diced
½ a cucumber - peeled and diced
½ a red onion - diced
1 tbsp of olive oil
1 tsp of lemon juice
Salt and black pepper to taste

1. Mix the ingredients in a salad bowl and toss together well.

Serves 1-2

SIDES & SUNDRIES

INDIAN MUSHROOM RICE

I'm using ordinary white mushrooms in this recipe, and it still tastes great, but you can mix up the varieties with oyster, cremini, or shiitake. It works well with any kind of rice, but a favourite of mine is basmati, which is a traditional Indian option.

180g (approx 1 cup) of basmati rice
4 mushrooms - diced
1 onion - diced
2 tbsp of olive oil
2 garlic cloves - crushed and chopped
½ tsp of ground cumin
1 tsp of ground turmeric
1 tsp of paprika
2 tbsp of fresh coriander - chopped
1 pint (approx 2 cups) of boiling water with a (gluten-free) vegetable stock cube
Salt and pepper to taste

1. Fry the onion, mushrooms, and garlic in olive oil in a saucepan until soft.
2. Add the spices, salt and pepper, and rice and coat well. Add the stock and bring to the boil, stirring well.
3. Cover with a lid and simmer on a low heat for 20 minutes. Don't be tempted to open the lid!
4. Turn off the heat and steam the rice for another few minutes, then mix in the coriander and serve.

Serves 2-4

Garnish
Fresh coriander - chopped

MIDDLE EASTERN POTATOES

Sick of plain old roast potatoes? Well, look no further. This is an easy way to spice them up, and it's a great alternative accompaniment to a curry instead of rice.

continued...

Middle Eastern Potatoes continued...

2 medium potatoes - cut into chunks
1 green pepper - sliced finely
1 red onion - sliced finely
1 red pepper - sliced finely
5 tbsp of olive oil
1 tsp of ground cumin
2 tsp of paprika
1 tsp of ground turmeric
1 tsp of ground coriander
Salt and pepper to taste

1. Add the olive oil, peppers, onion, cumin, coriander, paprika, turmeric, and salt and pepper to a baking dish and mix well.
2. Put the potatoes in a saucepan of boiling water. Turn the heat low and simmer for 3 minutes. Drain and add to the dish, mixing well again to cover the potatoes in oil and spices.
3. Cook in a preheated oven at 180°C for 35 to 45 minutes until the potatoes are cooked inside and crispy on the outside.

Serves 2-4

VEGETABLE PILAF

You can use any veggies that take your fancy in this recipe, and if you have any leftovers from my caramelised roast vegetable recipe (see Sides & Sundries), chuck them in the pot, and they'll work great. Wonderful as a side dish or its very own meal in a bowl.

180g (approx 1 cup) of rice
1 spring onion - sliced
2 large tomatoes - skinned and diced
1 red pepper - diced
1 green pepper - diced
2 tbsp of olive oil
2 garlic cloves - crushed and chopped
1 pint (approx 2 cups) of boiling water with a (gluten-free) vegetable stock cube
2 tsp of paprika
Salt and pepper to taste

Garnish
Flat-leaf parsley - chopped

1. Fry the onion and peppers in the olive oil in a saucepan until soft.
2. Add the garlic, paprika, and rice and mix well. Then add the stock, tomatoes, and salt and pepper and bring to the boil, stirring well.
3. Cover with a lid and simmer on a low heat for 20 minutes.
4. Turn off the heat and steam the rice for another few minutes then fluff up with a fork. Garnish with flat-leaf parsley and serve hot or as a cold rice salad.

Serves 2-4

CHEESY POTATO BAKE

I've listed this recipe as a side dish, but I often eat a whole plateful with just some baby rocket leaves or boiled peas. It's one of those comfort foods that give you a hug in a dish. If you don't want to use the cheese it will still taste lush.

2 medium potatoes - sliced thinly
1 red onion - sliced
½ tsp of dried thyme
5 tbsp of olive oil
2 tsp of paprika
200g (approx 1½ cups) of vegan cheddar-style cheese - grated
½ tbsp of garlic powder
Salt and pepper to taste

1. Add 4 tbsp of olive oil, thyme, paprika, garlic powder, and salt and pepper to a baking dish and mix well.
2. Add the potatoes to a saucepan of boiling water, turn the heat down, and simmer for 3 minutes. Drain and add to the baking dish.
3. In the meantime, fry the onion in 1 tbsp of olive oil.
4. Add the onions to the dish and mix everything together well so the potatoes are coated in herbs, spices, and oil.
5. Cook in a preheated oven at 180°C for 25 minutes. Add the cheese on top and a further drizzle of olive oil and bake for another 10 to 15 minutes until the cheese is bubbling and the edges are browned.

Serves 2-4

BBQ MUSHROOMS

The great thing about oyster mushrooms is they're very meaty in texture, and this recipe is similar to pulled pork. You could also replace the mushrooms with a can of drained jackfruit as a variation. Use as an accompaniment to a main meal or in a wrap or sandwich.

continued...

Bbq Mushrooms continued...

8 large oyster mushrooms - sliced or shredded
2 tsp of paprika
1 tsp of dried oregano
½ tsp of chipotle chilli flakes or smoked paprika
½ tsp of garlic powder
½ tsp of onion powder
2 tbsp of olive oil
Salt and pepper to taste

1. Add the mushrooms to a baking tray lined with baking paper
2. Mix the rest of the ingredients together and pour over the mushrooms. Mix well to coat.
3. Bake at 180°C for 30 minutes until the mushrooms have dried out and are slightly crispy.

Serves 2-4

VERMICELLI RICE

This is a traditional Turkish side dish, but I can actually eat a whole bowl on its own, hot or cold. It spices up plain rice into something a little bit more special.

180g (approx 1 cup) of rice
1 pint (approx 2 cups) of boiling water with a (gluten-free) vegetable stock cube
3 tbsp of (gluten-free) vermicelli noodles - broken into 1 inch pieces
1 tbsp of olive oil
1 tbsp of vegan butter
Salt and pepper to taste

1. Heat the butter and oil in a saucepan and add the vermicelli. Stir for a few minutes until it's golden, but make sure it doesn't burn.
2. Add the rice and stir for a few minutes to make sure everything's coated in oil and butter.
3. Add the stock and salt and pepper and bring to the boil, stirring well.
4. Cover with a lid and simmer on a low heat for 20 minutes.
5. Turn off the heat and steam the rice for another few minutes, then mix and serve.

Serves 2-4

SEXY CABBAGE

Poor cabbage gets a bit of a rough deal. It's probably best known as an accompaniment to a roast dinner, smothered in gravy, or grated into coleslaw. It's generally thought of as a bland veg that's well known for inflicting windyness on people. But cabbage is actually pretty cool. Researchers have found that it has unique cancer-preventing properties, especially in relation to colon, bladder, and prostate cancer. It's richer in vitamin C than oranges and has high levels of sulphur, which helps fight infections and ulcers. Because of these great properties, it's long been used for cleansing the body of free radicals and toxins. So isn't it about time we started sexing it up a bit?

½ a medium white cabbage – sliced
1 onion – sliced
2 garlic cloves – sliced
2 tsp of paprika
2 medium-sized tomatoes – skinned and diced
3 tbsp of olive oil for frying (this will also make the dressing)
Salt and pepper to taste

1. Steam the cabbage until it's soft.
2. Fry the onion and garlic in a saucepan with olive oil until soft and golden.
3. Add the chopped tomatoes and their juice, salt and pepper, and paprika, stirring well.
4. Drain the cabbage and add to the saucepan. Mix everything together, turn to a low heat, and cover with a lid. Cook for 5 minutes.
5. Serve hot or cold.

Serves 2-4

HERBY POTATO WEDGES

It only takes a few minutes of preparation to turn a bland potato into something sparkly. These easy peasy wedges will zing up your spuds in no time!

continued...

Herby Potato Wedges continued...

2 medium potatoes – cut into wedges
4 tbsp of olive oil
2 tsp of paprika
Dried oregano
Garlic powder

1. Put the potatoes in a saucepan of boiling water. Turn the heat low and simmer for 3 minutes.
2. Mix the olive oil and paprika in a baking dish.
3. Drain the potatoes and add to the dish, coating them well in the oil mix.
4. Sprinkle the potatoes with oregano and garlic powder and another drizzle of oil before baking in a preheated oven at 180°C for 35 to 40 minutes until the wedges are crispy.

Serves 2

CARAMELISED ROAST VEGETABLES

Roasting veggies is a sure way to add a bit of excitement to your diet. The only key ingredient here is when roasting them, make sure the oven's really hot when you start, and turn them frequently throughout so they're evenly coated in the juices and the heat is distributed, and they need to be roughly the same size.

If you have leftovers, use them in a frittata, or add them to a salad or soup the next day. I'm using vegan feta cheese, but feel free to add any vegan cheese or even omit it entirely. Roasting the garlic in its skin transforms the flavour from pungent to deliciously sweet.

1 large red onion
8 garlic cloves – in their skins
1 green pepper
1 red pepper
1 yellow pepper
1 aubergine
1 courgette (zucchini)
4 large mushrooms – quartered
2 tbsp of maple syrup
5 tbsp of olive oil
2 tbsp of (gluten-free/vegan) balsamic vinegar
1 tbsp of dried thyme
Salt and pepper to taste

Garnish
Flat-leaf parsley – chopped
Vegan feta cheese – diced **optional*

1. Cut the veggies into 1 inch chunks then add to a large baking tray.
2. In a separate bowl mix the other ingredients and pour over the veggies. Toss well so everything is coated.

continued...

Caramelised Roast Vegetables continued...

3. Cook in a preheated oven at 200°C for 35 to 45 minutes until the vegetables are soft and golden, turning them once or twice during cooking.
4. Sprinkle with feta and parsley and serve.

Serves 4

CORIANDER CARROTS

The Middle East meets North Africa in this harmonious mix of sweet and savoury flavours. I can eat a bowlful of these on their own, but they go well with couscous salad or golden turmeric rice (see recipes in Sumptuous Salads and Sides & Sundries) or a veggie tagine.

2 carrots - peeled and cut into batons 1 cm thick
1½ tbsp of ground coriander
1 tsp of garlic powder
1 tsp of paprika
¼ tsp of nutmeg
3 tbsp of olive oil
Zest of half an orange
Salt and pepper to taste

Garnish
Fresh coriander - chopped

1. Mix the oil, herbs and spices, orange zest, and salt and pepper in a small baking dish. Add the carrots and mix well to coat them evenly.
2. Roast in a preheated oven at 200°C for 15 minutes, then remove from the oven and mix the carrots around in the oil again. Bake for another 15 minutes until the carrots are tender.

Serves 2-4

MEDITERRANEAN GREEN BEANS

This easy way of cooking green beans can be found all around the Med. The secret is in the simplicity and fresh ingredients. Traditionally in Turkey these beans would be eaten at room temperature or cold, so it's also great as a salad or meze. I'm using flat beans, but feel free to use any green beans you prefer.

500g (approx 3 cups) of flat green beans - cut into 3 inch pieces
3 garlic cloves - sliced
3 large tomatoes - peeled and diced
½ a red onion - diced
¼ tsp of salt
¼ tsp of dried thyme
1 tsp of paprika
1 tsp of sugar *optional*
½ pint (approx 1 cup) of water
3 tbsp of olive oil
Pepper to taste

1. Fry the onions and tomatoes in olive oil for a few minutes.
2. Add the rest of the ingredients (there should be just enough water to cover the beans). Cover and simmer on a low heat for 20 to 25 minutes, or until the beans are soft.
3. Serve with a dollop of vegan yoghurt or crusty (gluten-free) bread to soak up the juices.

Serves 2-4

MINTED POTATOES

I eat potatoes a *lot*, and I'm a pretty minty girl, too! This dish is a great way to combine simplicity with full-on, refreshing flavour. Keeping the potato skins on while cooking means they'll retain more beneficial flavonoids and fibre, so it's up to you if you want to peel them.

continued...

Minted Potatoes continued...

2 medium potatoes - chopped into small cubes
1 red onion - diced
1 green pepper - diced
1 tbsp of dried mint
3 tbsp of olive oil
Salt and pepper to taste

1. Add the potatoes to a pan of boiling water and then simmer on a low heat for 15 to 20 minutes until they're soft.
2. In the meantime, fry the onion and pepper in 1 tbsp of olive oil for 5 minutes until soft and golden.
3. Drain the potatoes and add to a bowl. Add the onion, remaining olive oil, mint, and salt and pepper and toss well. Serve hot or cold.

Serves 2-4

FRIED AUBERGINE WITH TOMATO SALSA

Aubergine, also known as eggplant, can range in colour from light purple mixed with cream to almost black. In the Med they're used in every possible way you can think of: stuffed, in soups and casseroles, in rice, or as a dip.

Aubergines do soak up a lot of oil when frying, and one way to combat this is to sprinkle salt on them prior to cooking, which draws out the moisture, then pat them dry with kitchen paper. You can also bake them instead of frying, which will use less oil (see recipe for Moussaka in Light Bites & Main Meals).

3 large aubergines - cut into slices 1 cm thick
Olive oil for frying

For the tomato salsa
3 tomatoes - grated with juice
1 garlic clove - crushed and chopped
¼ tsp of chilli flakes
Salt and pepper to taste
Olive oil for frying

Garnish
Flat-leaf parsley - chopped

1. Cook the tomato sauce by mixing the ingredients in a saucepan and simmering on a low heat for 5 minutes.
2. Heat the oil in a frying pan. When it's very hot add the aubergines and fry in batches until tender and golden.
3. Remove the aubergine from the oil with a slotted spoon and place on a plate covered with kitchen paper to soak up any excess oil.
4. Serve with the salsa or BBQ dip (see recipe in Meze & Dips) or a dollop of vegan yoghurt.

Serves 2-4

MAPLE SPROUTS

Sprouts are one of those much-hated veggies that are usually relegated to the once-a-year Christmas appearance. I have to admit, I didn't like them until about ten years ago, but I think that was because I'd been scarred by bland, boiled-to-death boringness. This recipe turns their bitterness into something sweet and delicious. And hopefully their full sprout glory will shine!

Serves 4

500g (approx 5 cups) of Brussels sprouts – cut in half (stems and loose leaves trimmed off)
1 tsp of paprika
2 tbsp of maple syrup
4 tbsp of olive oil
Salt and pepper to taste

1. In a bowl mix the sprouts, paprika, olive oil, and salt and pepper and coat evenly.
2. Spread the sprouts on a baking tray in a single layer and bake in a preheated oven at 200°C for 15 minutes, flipping them over once during cooking. Then drizzle over the maple syrup and bake for a further 5 to 10 minutes until the sprouts are tender on the inside and caramelised on the outside.

GOLDEN TURMERIC RICE

Adding just one spice when cooking is a super easy way of giving your rice an extra oomph. I often have this with chilli or curries. You could also add some raisins and crushed, raw pistachios for a sweeter, more Middle Eastern-style pilaf.

Serves 2-4

continued...

Golden Turmeric Rice continued...

180g (approx 1 cup) of basmati rice
½ tsp of ground turmeric
1 garlic clove - crushed and chopped
1 pint (approx 2 cups) of boiling water with a (gluten-free) vegetable stock cube
1 tbsp of olive oil
Salt and pepper to taste

1. Fry the garlic in olive oil in a saucepan until soft and golden. Add the rice and turmeric and stir until the rice is coated.
2. Add the stock and salt and pepper then bring to the boil, stirring well.
3. Cover with a lid and simmer on a low heat for 20 minutes. Don't be tempted to open the lid!
4. Turn off the heat and steam the rice for another few minutes, then fluff up with a fork.

POTATO CAKES

There's no end to the amazingness of this versatile veg, and these easy potato cakes make a delicious light lunch with salad or a side dish.

2 medium potatoes - cut into small chunks
1 large carrot - sliced finely
1 large spring onion - sliced finely
1 or 2 garlic cloves - crushed and chopped
2 tbsp of flat-leaf parsley - chopped
Olive oil for frying
Salt and pepper to taste

1. Add the carrot and potatoes to a saucepan and cover with boiling water. Simmer on a low heat for 15 to 20 minutes, or until they're soft.
2. In the meantime, fry the spring onion and garlic with a little olive oil until soft.
3. Drain the potatoes and add back to the empty saucepan. Add the onion, garlic, parsley, and salt and pepper, mixing well, and mash until everything is smooth.
4. Wait until the potato mix is cool enough to handle and scoop out enough for a single potato cake. Shape in your hand and repeat for further cakes.
5. Fry the potato cakes in olive oil until they're crispy on the outside.

Serves 2-4

QUICK PARMESAN

This is a quick parmesan alternative that's great sprinkled on soups or salads, but I also use it a lot as a topping for baked dishes to give them that extra crunchy, cheesy twist. I make a batch and keep it in a glass jar in the fridge, and it lasts well for months.

150g (approx 1 cup) of raw cashew nuts
3 tbsp of nutritional yeast
1 tsp of garlic powder
1 tsp of onion powder

1. Blitz all the ingredients in a blender until you have a coarse powder.

ONION GRAVY

Vegan roast dinners need an equally fab accompaniment. This sauce is packed with flavour and so quick. If you don't want to use red wine, you can just replace it with more stock, or, as I like to do, use the juice and grated zest from one orange instead to make a lovely citrus gravy. It goes well with pies, vegan bangers and mash, or any other must-have-gravy dishes.

Makes approx 1 pint of gravy

1 pint (approx 2 cups) of boiling water with a (gluten-free) vegetable stock cube
¼ pint (approx ½ cup) of vegan red wine
½ tsp of dried thyme
1 tsp of paprika
½ tsp of tomato puree
¼ tsp of garlic powder
½ a red onion - diced
2½ tbsp of cornflour
4 tbsp of water
Olive oil for frying
Salt and pepper to taste

1. Fry the onion in a little olive oil until soft and caramelized.
2. Add the stock, wine, thyme, paprika, tomato puree, garlic powder, and salt and pepper. Bring to the boil, then cover and simmer for 10 minutes.
3. Mix the cornflour and water together until the flour has dissolved into a thick paste. Add the flour mix to the pan and stir on a medium heat until the gravy thickens. Repeat with a little more cornflour if the consistency is too thin for you.

LIGHT BITES & MAIN MEALS

CAULIFLOWER MINCEMEAT

I'm adding this recipe at the beginning of this section because I use it in some of the dishes that follow. It's dead easy to make, super tasty, and such a versatile addition to your cooking collection that can be added to pies, pizza, tacos, pasta, and much more. I often do a big batch and then split it up into portions and freeze it until I need it.

1 medium-sized head of cauliflower – chopped into small chunks
3 tbsp of tomato puree
1½ tbsp of (gluten-free) soya sauce or tamari
1 tsp of smoked paprika
½ tsp of chipotle chilli flakes
2 tsp of paprika
2 tsp of dried oregano
1 tsp of garlic powder
1 tsp of onion powder
Salt and pepper to taste

1. Put all the ingredients into a food processor and blitz into a coarse, mince-like blend.
2. Line a large baking tray with baking paper and spread the mixture out evenly on top.
3. Cook in a preheated oven at 180°C for 20 minutes and then stir the mixture before baking again for a further 20 minutes, or until the mince is cooked through and dried enough.
4. Use or freeze as required.

MANGO AND SWEET POTATO MASALA

I LOVE mangoes! They're great on their own or in smoothies, and their sweet, creamy texture lends itself really well to this mixture of Sri Lankan and Indian cooking. They're also high in fibre and antioxidants. To check if they're ripe, give them a gentle squeeze, and they should be slightly soft to the touch. Let's share the mango love as you check out this aromatic recipe with a velvety smoothness.

continued...

Mango And Sweet Potato Masala continued...

1 fresh, ripe mango - peeled and diced
1 large sweet potato - diced
1 red onion - diced
2 garlic cloves - crushed and chopped
½ pint (approx 1 cup) water
½ pint (approx 1 cup) of coconut milk
50g (approx ½ cup) of frozen peas
1 tsp of tomato puree
1 chilli - deseeded and chopped
1 tbsp of garam masala
½ tsp of ground turmeric
1 tsp of paprika

2 tsp of ground coriander
2 tbsp of coconut oil for frying
Salt and pepper to taste

1. Fry the onion in coconut oil for 5 minutes until it's soft and golden.
2. Add the rest of the ingredients then bring to the boil. Cover and simmer for 20 minutes. Serve with golden turmeric rice (see recipe in Sides & Sundries) or basmati rice.

Serves 2

BASIL PESTO PASTA

A little of this veganised Italian recipe goes a long way because the basil is powerfully aromatic. You could do a mix and match here and swap half the basil for another green herb or leafy veg like baby spinach, baby rocket, or flat-leaf parsley. Any excess can be stored in a glass jar in the fridge for several days.

For the pesto
50g (approx ½ cup) of raw pine nuts
2 garlic cloves - peeled
40g (approx 2 cups) of fresh basil leaves
65g (approx ½) cup of vegan parmesan-style cheese (or any vegan hard cheese)
3 tbsp of nutritional yeast
6 tbsp of olive oil
Salt and pepper to taste

For the pasta
200g of (gluten-free) spaghetti

1. Cook the pasta according to the packet instructions.
2. In the meantime, add all the pesto ingredients to a food processor and blend into a coarse paste.
3. Drain the pasta and place back in saucepan. Add as much pesto as you prefer and toss until mixed.

Serves 2-4

SOUTHERN FRIED TOFU NUGGETS

These are herby, crispy, and pack a giant flavour punch. It's a little bit fiddly due to the dredging/coating process, but I promise the effort will be worth it. I'm calling them nuggets, but you can cut the tofu into any shape you like – wedges, slabs, fingers, it's all good!

For the tofu marinade

500g block of firm tofu - drained and pressed and cut into fingers 1½ cm thick
½ pint (approx 1 cup) of water with a (gluten-free) vegetable stock cube dissolved in it
1 tbsp of (gluten-free) soya sauce or tamari
½ tsp of vegan Dijon mustard

For the milk mixture

¼ pint (approx ½ cup) of soya milk
1 tsp of apple cider vinegar or lemon juice

For the breading mixture

130g (approx 1 cup) of cornflour
2 tbsp of nutritional yeast
¼ tsp of ground black pepper
¼ tsp of salt
1 tbsp of paprika
1 tsp of dried thyme
1 tsp of garlic powder
1 tsp of onion powder
1 tsp of dried oregano
¼ tsp of chipotle chilli flakes
¼ tsp of dried rosemary
1 tsp of ground turmeric
½ tsp of dried parsley

For the dredging

65g (approx ½ cup) of cornflour

1. Prepare the different sections of ingredients and set aside.
2. Marinate the pressed tofu in the fridge for at least 4 hours but preferably overnight. Then drain and pat dry with a kitchen towel.
3. Coat the tofu in the dredging flour, then submerge in the milk mixture. Shake off the excess liquid and coat in the breading mixture. Repeat for all the tofu.
4. Shallow fry in olive oil for 3 to 5 minutes on each side until crispy. Serve with BBQ dip or ranch-style mayo (see recipes in Meze & Dips).

Serves 2

MOUSSAKA

One of the exciting things about being vegan is using your creativity to veganise recipes. When I was a kid my parents used to cook the meat variety of moussaka all the time, but I missed this deliciously rich taste of the Med, so here's my adapted version with a secret ingredient to give it some extra zing: cinnamon! Traditionally, this is served with a white sauce on top, but I prefer it without. If you want to add a white sauce, check out the sauce in my oven-baked pasta recipe (see Light Bites & Main Meals).

Because aubergines soak up a lot of oil when frying, I'm oven roasting them instead, but feel free to fry them if you prefer.

Variation: You can also replace the aubergines with courgettes (zucchinis) or partly cooked and sliced potatoes.

600g (approx 4 cups) of (gluten-free) soya mince or cauliflower mince (see recipe in Light Bites & Main Meals)
5 aubergines - sliced 1 cm thick
4 mushrooms - diced
2 onions - diced
3 garlic cloves - crushed and chopped
400g can of tomatoes
2 tsp of tomato puree
2 tbsp of dried oregano
2 tsp of paprika
¼ tsp of dried cinnamon
1 pint (approx 2 cups) of boiling water with a (gluten-free) vegetable stock cube
350g (approx 4 cups) of vegan cheese - grated
Olive oil
Salt and pepper to taste

1. Place the aubergine slices flat on a large baking tray (you may need to do this in batches). Brush with olive oil and bake in a preheated oven at 220°C for 10 to 15 minutes until the tops brown. Turn the slices over, brush with more oil, and cook for a further 10 minutes. They should be soft and golden when they're ready.
2. In the meantime, fry the onions in olive oil in a large saucepan until soft and golden. Add the mushrooms and garlic and fry for a few minutes.
3. Add the mince and mix for a few minutes then add in the tomatoes, cinnamon, stock, paprika, oregano, tomato puree, and salt and pepper and stir well. Cover and simmer for 20 minutes. If the sauce gets too dry add a little more water.
4. When the aubergines are cooked, we're ready to start assembling the moussaka. In a deep baking dish add layers of alternating sauce and aubergines with a sprinkling of cheese in between. Top with more cheese and a drizzle of olive oil.
5. Bake in the oven for 35 minutes, until the top is crispy and golden and the inside is bubbling. Perfect served with a crisp green salad or roast potatoes.

Serves 4

SPANISH FRITTATA

This recipe uses silken tofu, which has a higher liquid content that makes it softer. You can use any veggies you like, but I'm incorporating more traditional Spanish omelette-style ingredients. This can be served hot or cold and is more filling than it looks.

200g of extra-firm silken tofu - drained and pressed
200ml (approx ¾ cup) of water
2 mushrooms - diced
1 garlic clove - pressed and chopped
1 green pepper - diced
1 red onion - diced
1 medium potato - peeled, diced, and boiled until soft
55g (approx ½ cup) of chickpea flour
2 tbsp of flat-leaf parsley - chopped
2 tbsp of cornflour
1 tsp of ground turmeric
1 tbsp of nutritional yeast
100g (approx 1 cup) of vegan cheese - grated
Salt and pepper to taste
Olive oil

1. Add the tofu, water, garlic, chickpea flour, parsley, cornflour, ground turmeric, nutritional yeast, and salt and pepper to a food processor. Blend for a couple of minutes until it becomes a thin batter-like consistency.
2. In a frying pan with a grill-proof handle, fry the mushrooms, onion, and pepper in olive oil until soft. Add the potatoes and heat through.
3. Pour over the frittata batter and jiggle the pan so it coats the veggies. Turn the heat to low and cook for 3 to 5 minutes.
4. Place the pan under a low-setting grill for 5 to 8 minutes until it starts to set.
5. Add the cheese on top and a drizzle of olive oil then grill for another 3 to 5 minutes until the top is firm and bubbling. Cut into wedges and serve.

Serves 2-4

TURKISH CASSEROLE

This is a simple Turkish dish that's high in flavour but low in prep work. I love using oyster mushrooms because they're such a meaty veg, but feel free to use regular mushrooms if you prefer.

1 aubergine - diced
1 green pepper - diced
1 onion - diced
3 oyster mushrooms - diced
2 garlic cloves - pressed and chopped
1 large tomato - diced
2 tsp of dried oregano
1 tsp of paprika
¼ tsp of chilli flakes
¼ tsp of ground black pepper
¾ pint (approx 1½ cups) of boiling water with a (gluten-free) vegetable stock cube
100g (approx 1 cup) of vegan cheese - grated
Salt to taste
Olive oil

1. In a saucepan fry the aubergine, pepper, and onion in olive oil for a few minutes. Add the mushrooms and fry for a couple of minutes until browned.
2. Add the tomato, garlic, stock, herbs, and salt and pepper, then cover and simmer for 15 minutes.
3. Spoon into bowls, add the cheese on top, and place under a grill until the cheese is bubbling. Serve with golden turmeric rice (see recipe in Sides & Sundries).

Serves 2

ONION BHAJIS WITH TOMATO CHUTNEY

I'm a huge fan of onion bhajis, and this easy recipe gives you a really crispy and flavoursome taste of India that's ideal for a lunchtime snack, a light dinner, or eaten cold on a picnic. If you want a slightly sweeter taste, then use red onions.

For the bhajis
2 large onions - sliced
1 green pepper - sliced finely
200g (approx 2 cups) of chickpea flour
3 tbsp of fresh coriander - chopped
1 tbsp of paprika
1 tbsp of ground turmeric
2 tsp of ground cumin
1 tbsp of dried coriander
1 tbsp of coriander seeds
½ tsp of chilli flakes
¼ pint (approx ½ cup) of water
Salt and pepper to taste
Sunflower oil for deep frying

For the tomato chutney
½ a red onion - diced
2 large tomatoes - peeled and diced
¼ of a large cucumber - peeled and diced
1 to 2 tbsp of fresh coriander - chopped
Juice of half a lemon
Sprinkling of black pepper
Salt to taste

1. Mix the tomato chutney ingredients in a bowl. Stir and set aside.
2. Mix all the bhaji ingredients, except the oil and water, in a large bowl and make sure everything is evenly coated in flour and spices.
3. Add the water and mix until it becomes a thick, sticky batter. Let it sit for about 5 minutes. Add a little more water if necessary.
4. Heat the sunflower oil in a large saucepan, using enough to cover the bhajis. You can test whether the oil's hot enough by adding a piece of batter. If it sizzles, it's ready to go!
5. Take a heaped spoonful of the batter and mould into a dumpling size using a second spoon. Drop carefully into the oil, frying in batches of 4 to 5 at a time. Cook until crispy and golden, flipping them over to ensure both sides are cooked.
6. Drain them on kitchen paper to soak up excess oil. Serve hot or cold.

Serves 2-4

SALT-AND-PEPPER TOFU

This is one of my favourite Chinese recipes. Its full-on flavour turns the tofu into something really special. The salty, crispy-coated tofu mixed with the spicy, aromatic veggies is totally addictive.

500g block of firm tofu - drained and pressed and cut into small cubes
Olive oil

For the coating
½ tsp of ground Himalayan pink salt
½ tsp of ground black pepper
6 tbsp of cornflour
1 tsp of paprika

For the veg
2 spring onions - sliced
1 red chilli - sliced
1 green chilli - sliced
2 garlic cloves - sliced
1 tbsp of sesame oil

1. Mix the coating ingredients in a bowl. Add the tofu and mix until it's evenly coated.
2. Line a baking tray with greaseproof paper and brush on a thin coating of olive oil. Add the tofu to the tray, making sure it's evenly spaced out. Bake in a preheated oven at 220°C for 15 minutes then stir the tofu to mix. Bake for another 15 minutes until it's golden and crispy.
3. Just before the tofu is ready, fry the spring onions, chillies, and garlic in sesame oil until soft and golden. Serve on the side or sprinkle over the tofu.

Serves 2

RICH SPAGHETTI BOLOGNESE

This veganised version of the Italian classic that traditionally uses meat is rich in flavour and very meaty in consistency. It's my go-to weeknight recipe when I'm low on time but still want something satisfyingly delish!

Tip: You can replace the cauliflower mince with your favourite (gluten-free) soya mince or a can of drained and rinsed lentils.

200g of (gluten-free) spaghetti
150g (approx 1 cup) of cauliflower mince (see recipe in Light Bites & Main Meals)
1 onion - diced
2 mushrooms - diced
2 garlic cloves - crushed and chopped
1 small carrot - grated
2 tsp of tomato puree
400g can of tomatoes
½ pint (approx 1 cup) of water
2 tsp of paprika
2 tsp of dried oregano
2 tbsp of flat-leaf parsley - chopped
Salt and pepper to taste
Olive oil for frying

1. Cook the spaghetti in a saucepan according to the packet instructions.
2. Fry the onion in olive oil in a saucepan for 5 minutes until soft and golden. Add the mushrooms and garlic and fry for another few minutes.
3. Add the rest of the ingredients to the veggies. Cover and simmer for 20 minutes.
4. Drain the pasta and place back in the saucepan. Add the sauce and toss until mixed.

Serves 2

CANNELLINI BEAN FRITTERS

I love these served hot with a squeeze of lemon or a dollop of yoghurt and cucumber dip (see recipe in Meze & Dips). Any leftovers also go well added to a burrito or wrap.

continued...

Cannellini Bean Fritters continued...

400g can of cannellini beans - drained and rinsed
2 garlic cloves - crushed and chopped
1 spring onion - sliced
½ tsp of ground cumin
¼ tsp of chilli flakes
3 tbsp of fresh coriander - chopped
1 tbsp of cornflour
Salt and pepper to taste
Olive oil for frying
Cornflour for coating

1. Place the beans in a bowl and mash them until they resemble a thick paste consistency.
2. Fry the onion and garlic in a small amount of olive oil until soft and transfer to the bowl. Add the ground cumin, chilli, coriander, salt and pepper, and 1 tbsp of cornflour, and mix well. Take a small amount and make it into fritter-sized balls with your hand. Repeat for more fritters.
3. Coat them in cornflour and fry in olive oil over a medium heat until golden and crispy.

Makes approx 5 fritters

ASPARAGUS AND MUSHROOM RISOTTO

The ingredients might be basic, but the taste is anything but. Even if you omit the vegan cream and cheese, you'll still end up with a rich, mouthwatering meal that's completely worth the constant stirring and attention.

Serves 2-4

200g (approx 1 cup) of arborio rice
1½ pints (approx 3 cups) of boiling water with a (gluten-free) vegetable stock cube
3 oyster mushrooms - diced
1 spring onion - sliced
3 asparagus spears - sliced finely
2 garlic cloves - crushed and chopped
½ tsp of dried thyme
4 tbsp of soya cream
Salt and pepper to taste
Olive oil for frying

Garnish
Vegan cheese - grated
Flat-leaf parsley - chopped

1. Pour the boiled stock into a saucepan and keep on a low heat.
2. Fry the onion and mushrooms in olive oil in a saucepan for a few minutes until soft and golden. Add the garlic, thyme, asparagus, salt and pepper, and rice and stir well to allow the grains to coat thoroughly.
3. Ladle over just enough hot stock to cover the rice then simmer until most of the liquid has been absorbed. Repeat the process a ladleful at a time, stirring constantly until each ladleful is soaked up by the rice. It will take about 20 to 25 minutes to be fully cooked. If you run out of stock before the rice is ready add a little more boiled water.
4. Stir in the soya cream and heat through. Sprinkle with cheese and parsley and serve.

SCRAMBLED "EGGY" TOFU

If you're missing scrambled egg on a plant-based diet then this will give you a super eggy flavour packed full of protein. It's perfect for a light lunch or breakfast idea, and I sometimes bling it up with a handful of baby spinach leaves or spring onions.

200g of extra-firm silken tofu - drained and pressed
2 tbsp of nutritional yeast
½ tsp of ground turmeric
½ tsp of paprika
½ tsp of vegan Dijon mustard
1 tsp of garlic powder
½ tsp of onion powder
¼ tsp of kala namak (see Quick Tips)
1 tbsp of olive oil for frying
1 tbsp of vegan butter for frying
Salt and pepper to taste

Garnish
Sprinkling of black pepper
Flat-leaf parsley - chopped

1. Mash the tofu with a fork until it's a scrambled egg consistency. Add the rest of the ingredients, except for the oil and butter, and mix thoroughly.
2. Heat the butter and oil in a pan then add the tofu and fry on a medium heat for 5 minutes until hot, being careful not to break it up too much.

Serves 2

GREEK-STYLE SHEPHERD'S PIE

This is a variation of shepherd's pie which is topped with rice instead of mashed potatoes. A creamy yoghurt mix gives this a lovely tang. Serve with salad or veggies.

Variation: Use a can of drained and rinsed lentils instead of vegan mince.

180g (approx 1 cup) of rice
600g (approx 4 cups) of (gluten-free) soya mince or cauliflower mince (see recipe in Light Bites & Main Meals)
1 onion - diced
2 garlic cloves - crushed and chopped
2 carrots - sliced very finely
50g (about ½ cup) of frozen garden peas
1 pint (approx 2 cups) of boiling water with a (gluten-free) vegetable stock cube
2 tsp of tomato puree
1 tbsp of dried thyme
1½ tbsp of dried oregano
250g (approx 1 cup) of vegan yoghurt
200g (approx 1½ cups) of vegan cheese - grated
Olive oil
Salt and pepper to taste

1. Cook the rice according to the packet instructions.
2. In the meantime, fry the onion until soft and golden. Add the garlic and mince and stir for a few minutes.
3. Mix in the tomato puree, carrots, peas, thyme, oregano, salt and pepper, and stock. Cover and simmer for 20 minutes. If the sauce becomes too thick add a little more water. Pour into a deep oven dish and press flat.
4. Mix the cooked rice with the yoghurt and half of the cheese then spread over the mince. Press down then sprinkle the rest of the cheese on top and drizzle over olive oil. Cook in a preheated oven at 180°C for 25 to 30 minutes until the top is crispy and golden and the inside is bubbling.

Serves 2-4

TURKISH PIZZA

For an easy variation of Turkish pizza (lahmacun) without the faff of making dough, I'm using pre-bought gluten-free tortillas as the base. Feel free to use any (gluten-free) pizza base or flatbread you like. It's traditionally served with a drizzle of fresh lemon juice.

2 (gluten-free/vegan) tortillas or flatbread
300g (approx 2 cups) of cauliflower mince (see recipe in Light Bites & Main Meals)
½ a red onion - diced
1 green cubanelle pepper (or regular bell pepper) - diced
1 garlic clove - crushed and diced
1 large tomato - diced
¼ tsp of chilli flakes
¼ tsp of ground cumin
3 tbsp of flat-leaf parsley - chopped
¼ tsp of sumac *optional*
Tomato puree
Salt and pepper to taste
Olive oil

Garnish
Lemon wedges

1. Place the tortillas on a large baking tray or two smaller ones.
2. Mix the rest of the ingredients, apart from the tomato puree and olive oil, in a bowl.
3. Spread the tortillas with a thin layer of tomato puree. Add the topping from the bowl and spread out evenly.
4. Drizzle with olive oil and cook in a preheated oven at 180°C for 8 to 10 minutes. Squeeze a lemon wedge over the top and serve.

Serves 2

EASY LASAGNE

Traditionally, lasagne is topped with a white sauce, but if, like me, you can't be bothered with that fiddly stuff, then this version will give you all the scrummy taste but without the extra effort. If you want to top with white sauce check out my recipe for oven-baked pasta in Light Bites & Main Meals, and you'll find one there.

Tip: You can replace the cauliflower mince with your favourite (gluten-free) soya mince or a can of drained and rinsed lentils.

300g (approx 2 cups) of cauliflower mince (see recipe in Light Bites & Main Meals)
1 onion - diced
2 mushrooms - diced
1 garlic clove - crushed and chopped
1 small carrot - grated
400g can of tomatoes
½ pint (approx 1 cup) of water
2 tsp of paprika
2 tsp of fresh basil - chopped
2 tsp of dried oregano
½ tsp of chipotle chilli flakes
150g (approx 1½ cups) of vegan cheese - grated
8 sheets of (gluten-free) lasagne
Salt and pepper to taste
4 tbsp of quick parmesan (see recipe in Sides & Sundries)
Olive oil

1. Fry the onion in olive oil for 5 minutes until soft and golden. Add the mushrooms and garlic and fry until soft. Add all the other ingredients, apart from the lasagne, vegan cheese, and quick parmesan. Cover and simmer for 20 minutes.
2. To assemble the lasagne, pour half the sauce into the dish and sprinkle with a little of the vegan cheese. Place 4 sheets of lasagne on top. Add half of the remaining sauce then cover it with the rest of the sheets. Pour the rest of the sauce on top and press down so it covers the pasta sheets.
3. Sprinkle over the remaining vegan cheese and then top with quick vegan parmesan and a drizzle of olive oil.
4. Bake in a preheated oven at 180°C for 25 to 30 minutes until the top is bubbling and golden.

Serves 2

CAULIFLOWER AND BROCCOLI CHEESE

I know I'm biased but this recipe is so delish! And the good thing is, even if you don't want to use any vegan cheese, it's still fantastically cheesy without it. I like to split the serving in half and serve in two individual dishes, but feel free to cook it as one whole dish.

½ a medium head of cauliflower - cut into florets
½ a medium head of broccoli - cut into florets
100g (approx 1 cup) of vegan cheese - grated

For the sauce
1 pint (approx 2 cups) of soya milk (or almond milk)
¼ tsp of ground turmeric
½ tsp of vegan Dijon mustard
1 (gluten-free) vegetable stock cube
1 tsp of vegan butter
½ tsp of garlic powder
½ tsp of onion powder
½ tsp of chives *optional*
2 tbsp of cornflour
3 tbsp of nutritional yeast
1 tbsp of olive oil
Salt and pepper to taste

For the topping
Quick parmesan (see recipe in Sides & Sundries)
Dusting of paprika

1. Steam the cauliflower and broccoli for 10 minutes until it's tender then add to a baking dish. Top with the vegan cheese.
2. Add all the sauce ingredients to a saucepan and whisk on a medium heat until it comes to the boil and thickens.
3. Pour the sauce over the cauliflower and broccoli. Sprinkle with quick parmesan and a dusting of paprika. Drizzle olive oil on top then cook in a preheated oven at 180°C for 20 minutes.

Serves 2

NO-FUSS PAELLA

If you want all the vibrant colour and smoky taste of the classic Spanish dish but without the fuss of having to use special rice, a paella pan, and attend to it constantly while it's cooking, then look no further.

180g (approx 1 cup) of long-grain rice
1 pint (approx 2 cups) of boiling water with a (gluten-free) vegetable stock cube
½ a red onion – diced
½ a red pepper – diced
½ a green pepper – diced
2 garlic cloves – crushed and chopped
1 large tomato – diced
1 tsp of smoked paprika
1 tsp of paprika
1 tsp of ground turmeric
1 tsp of dried thyme
50g (approx ½ cup) of frozen peas
25g (approx ½ cup) of frozen green beans
Salt and pepper to taste
Olive oil for frying

Garnish
Flat-leaf parsley – chopped
Lemon wedges

1. Fry the onion and peppers in olive oil in a saucepan for a few minutes. Add the rice and spices and stir to coat everything in the oil.
2. Add the rest of the ingredients, then cover and simmer for 20 minutes.
3. When it's ready, give it one final stir to mix through. Serve topped with parsley and a squeeze of lemon juice.

Serves 2-4

STICKY BBQ TOFU

Tofu often gets a bad rap but I think it's totally misunderstood. When I first went vegan I didn't have a clue what to do with tofu, and although it's bland on its own, in the same way pasta and potatoes are, it's so versatile and adaptable with marinades, sauces, and coatings. This wonderfully smoky, sticky dish will liven up your tofu with very little effort.

500g block of firm tofu – drained and pressed and cut into 1 cm slices
Olive oil

For the sauce
2 tbsp of tomato puree
4 tbsp of (gluten-free) soya sauce or tamari
3 tbsp of maple syrup
¼ pint (approx ½ cup) of water
¼ tsp of chipotle chilli flakes
3 tbsp of olive oil
1 tbsp of cornflour
1 garlic clove – pressed and chopped
Salt and pepper to taste

1. Mix all the sauce ingredients, apart from the cornflour, in a baking dish. Add the tofu and arrange evenly spaced out. Spoon the sauce on top and marinate in the fridge for between 30 minutes and 4 hours. Afterwards, pour the marinade into a saucepan with the cornflour. Stir to mix and set aside.
2. Line a baking tray with baking paper and brush on a thin coating of olive oil. Arrange the tofu in planks on the paper, evenly spaced out. The tofu should still be covered with a bit of residual marinade, but if not, brush the surface with the sauce. Bake in a preheated oven at 220°C for 15 minutes.
3. Flip the tofu over, brush a little more marinade on top, and bake for a further 10 minutes, or until the edges brown and crispen up.
4. When the tofu is ready, whisk the sauce on a medium heat until it boils and thickens up. Pour on top and serve with speedy Asian noodles (see recipe in Light Bites & Main Meals).

Serves 2-4

SPEEDY ASIAN NOODLES

Who needs a takeaway with this combo of Asian flavours and a super-speedy recipe that takes around 15 minutes start to finish? If you want to swap the vermicelli rice noodles for another variety of (gluten-free/vegan) noodle, go right ahead – you just might have to adjust their cooking time.

200g of vermicelli rice noodles
150g (approx 1½ cups) of white cabbage – shredded
1 carrot – grated
1 or 2 spring onions – sliced finely
½ inch piece of root ginger – peeled and grated
2 garlic cloves – crushed and chopped
4 tbsp of (gluten-free) soya sauce or tamari
1 chilli – deseeded and chopped finely
1 tbsp of water
1 tbsp of sesame oil
Salt and pepper to taste
Olive oil for frying

1. In a small bowl mix the ginger, garlic, soya sauce, water, salt and pepper, and sesame oil and set aside.
2. Cook the noodles according to the packet instructions.
3. Fry the carrot, cabbage, chilli, and spring onions in olive oil until soft.
4. Add the sauce mix to the veggies and stir through.
5. Drain the noodles and add to the sauce and veggies. Mix well and serve.

Serves 2

CHILLI CON CARNE

For this timeless classic dish I'm using my cauliflower mince (see recipe in Light Bites & Main Meals), but feel free to use your favourite (gluten-free) soya mince, or swap the mince for lentils. It's got a full-bodied, wholesome flavour, and I love it served with golden turmeric rice (see recipe in Sides & Sundries) or roast potatoes.

300g (approx 2 cups) of cauliflower mince (see recipe)
1 onion - diced
2 garlic cloves - crushed and chopped
1 green pepper - diced
1 large carrot - grated
400g can of red kidney beans - drained and rinsed
400g can of chopped tomatoes
1 tbsp of dried oregano
½ tsp of ground cumin
¼ to ½ tsp of chipotle chilli flakes (or more, depending on the heat you like)
2 tsp of tomato puree
2 tsp of paprika
1 tbsp of (gluten-free/vegan) balsamic vinegar or lemon juice
¾ pint (approx 1½ cups) of boiled water with a (gluten-free) vegetable stock cube
2 tbsp of flat-leaf parsley - chopped
Salt and pepper to taste
Olive oil for frying

Garnish
Flat-leaf parsley - chopped

1. Fry the onion and pepper in olive oil for 5 minutes until soft.
2. Add the rest of the ingredients, except for the parsley, and bring to the boil. Simmer for 25 minutes.
3. Stir in the parsley and serve.

Serves 2-4

QUICK PITA PIZZA

We all live busy lives these days, and this easy pizza suggestion is ideal for quick lunch or light dinner. I'm using gluten-free pita bread, but feel free to use any kind of (gluten-free) tortilla or flatbread as the base. You can use any toppings you like, but here's my favourite twist on it...

2 (gluten-free) pita breads - cut in half lengthwise
2 spring onions - sliced
1 green pepper - diced
2 large tomatoes - sliced
1 tsp of dried oregano
100g (approx 1 cup) of vegan cheese - grated
Tomato puree
Salt and pepper to taste
Olive oil

1. Spread the pita bread with a thin layer of tomato puree. Top with the veggies, oregano, seasoning, and cheese, then drizzle over some olive oil.
2. Cook in a preheated oven at 180°C for 8 to 10 minutes.

Serves 1-2

SIMPLE GARLIC PASTA

Here's an easy Cypriot recipe that can be on the table in the time it takes to cook the pasta. The mint gives it a hint of Middle Eastern flavour, and it's coated in lush olive oil.

200g of (gluten-free) pasta
2 or 3 garlic cloves - crushed and chopped
2 spring onions - sliced
1 to 2 tsp of dried mint
3 tbsp of olive oil
Salt and pepper to taste

Garnish
Sprinkling of vegan cheese *optional*

1. Cook the pasta in a large saucepan according to the packet instructions.
2. Fry the garlic and spring onions in the oil for a few minutes.
3. Drain the pasta and place back in cooking pan. Add the mint, garlic, onions, and olive oil from the frying pan. Season and toss until mixed.

Serves 2-4

AUBERGINE PARMIGIANA

Even a few simple ingredients can create something heavenly, and this is my version of the Italian bake that's usually made with parmesan cheese. Because aubergines soak up a lot of oil when frying, I'm oven roasting them instead, but feel free to fry them if you prefer.

4 aubergines - sliced 1 cm thick
2 x 400g can of tomatoes
2 garlic cloves - diced
4 tbsp of flat-leaf parsley - chopped
200g (approx 1½ cups) of vegan cheese - grated
Salt and pepper to taste
Quick parmesan (see recipe in Sides & Sundries)
Olive oil

1. Place the aubergine slices flat on a large baking tray (you may need to do this in batches). Brush with olive oil and bake in a preheated oven at 220°C for 10 to 15 minutes until the tops brown. Turn the slices over, brush with more oil, and cook for a further 10 to 15 minutes. They should be soft and golden when they're ready.
2. Spoon half the tomatoes into the bottom of a baking dish. Top with a sprinkling of garlic, parsley, and quick parmesan, then layer on half of the aubergine slices. Add the rest of the tomatoes on top and sprinkle with the remaining garlic, parsley, and salt and pepper. Add the final layer of aubergines and press down so the sauce slightly covers the top of them.
3. Sprinkle with vegan cheese, more quick parmesan, and a drizzle of olive oil and bake at 180°C for 25 to 30 minutes, until the top is crispy and golden and the inside is bubbling.

Serves 2

SWEET AND SOUR TOFU

Hailed as a favourite Chinese dish for a good reason, this recipe does exactly what the name suggests and gives you a blast of sweet and sour satisfaction and crispy-coated tofu with every spoonful.

For the tofu
500g block of firm tofu - drained and pressed and cut into cubes
Olive oil
6 tbsp of cornflour
1 tsp of paprika

For the sauce
2 tbsp of tomato puree
4 tbsp of (gluten-free) soya sauce or tamari
3 tbsp of maple syrup
¼ pint (approx ½ cup) of water
1 tsp of white rice vinegar
2 tsp of cornflour
1 garlic clove - pressed and chopped
2 tsp of sesame seeds
Salt and pepper to taste

For the veggies
1 green pepper - diced
1 red pepper - diced
2 spring onions - diced
1 tbsp of sesame oil for frying

1. Mix all the sauce ingredients in a jug and set aside.
2. For the tofu, mix the cornflour and paprika in a bowl. Add the drained tofu and toss until it's evenly coated.
3. Line a baking tray with baking paper and brush on a thin coating of olive oil. Add the tofu, making sure it's evenly spaced out. Bake in a preheated oven at 220°C for 15 minutes, then stir the tofu around to make sure it's cooking evenly and bake for another 15 minutes until it's golden and crispy.
4. In the meantime, fry the onion, pepper, and garlic in the sesame oil until soft. Add the jug of sauce and stir on a medium heat until it thickens up. Pour on top of the baked tofu and serve with rice or noodles.

Serves 2

MOROCCAN CAULIFLOWER STEAKS

Yes, cauliflower can be bland on its own, but since being vegan I've discovered just what a wonder veg it actually is. You can turn it into rice, creamy sauces, and coat it with amazing flavours that transform something understated into a wow factor. Dusted with fragrant herbs and spices, this recipe is a meaty alternative to steak that will have even the cauliflower sceptics changing their minds.

1 large head of cauliflower - leaves removed and sliced into four 1 cm thick steaks
Drizzle of olive oil

For the spice mix
¼ tsp of ground cinnamon
1 tbsp of ground coriander
1 tsp of ground turmeric
1 tsp of ground cumin
¼ tsp of ground nutmeg
1 tbsp of paprika
1 tsp of smoked paprika
Salt and pepper to taste

1. Mix the spice ingredients in a bowl and then pat over both sides of the cauli steaks. Place them on a baking tray covered with baking paper.
2. Drizzle with a generous slug of olive oil and roast in a preheated oven at 200°C for 20 to 25 minutes until the steaks are tender inside and crispy on the outside. Spoon over the spice-infused cooking oil and serve with lemon tahini tip (see recipe in Meze & Dips).

Serves 2

LENTIL AND CHESTNUT GOULASH

Originating in Hungary, goulash is traditionally a stew of meat, veggies, and paprika. The oyster mushrooms and meaty chestnuts are the heart of this vegan version, and the citrus flavour is my little twist on things.

1 spring onion – sliced
2 garlic cloves – crushed and chopped
4 large oyster mushrooms (or regular mushrooms) – diced
150g (approx 1 cup) of pre-cooked and peeled chestnuts
Zest and juice of 1 orange
¼ pint (approx 1½ cups) of boiling water with a vegetable stock cube
1 large tomato – grated
2 tbsp of flat-leaf parsley – chopped
100g (approx ¼ cup) of red lentils
2 tsp of paprika
Salt and pepper to taste
Olive oil for frying

Garnish
Flat-leaf parsley – chopped

1. Fry the onion and mushrooms in olive oil in a saucepan for 5 minutes until soft and golden. Add the rest of the ingredients and then simmer for 25 minutes.
2. Sprinkle with parsley and serve with vermicelli rice (see recipe in Sides & Sundries).

Serves 2

BRAISED MINCE BOURGUIGNONNE

The traditional French bourguignonne is made with beef, but my vegan take on it is just as deeply flavoured as the original. It's a filling comfort dish which is ace served with mashed potatoes.

2 large oyster mushrooms - diced
1 red onion - diced
1 carrot - diced
2 garlic cloves - pressed and chopped
300g (approx 2 cups) of cauliflower mince (see recipe in Light Bites & Main Meals)
½ pint of boiling water with a (gluten-free) vegetable stock cube
¼ pint (approx ½ cup) of vegan red wine
1 tsp of tomato puree
1 tsp of dried thyme
2 tsp of paprika
¼ tsp of smoked paprika
2 bay leaves
2 tbsp of flat-leaf parsley - chopped
Salt and pepper to taste
Olive oil for frying

Garnish
Flat-leaf parsley - chopped

1. Fry the onion and mushrooms in olive oil in a saucepan for 5 minutes until browned.
2. Add the rest of the ingredients, then cover and simmer for 20 minutes. If the sauce becomes too thick add a little more water. Remove the bay leaves and serve.

Serves 2-4

POTATO-CRUST PIZZA

Yes, you *can* make pizza out of potatoes! It's incredibly simple and naturally gluten-free, and if you're a pizza lover I'm sure it won't disappoint.

1 batch of easy peasy spinach pesto (see recipe in Meze & Dips)
2 medium potatoes - peeled and diced
2 tomatoes - sliced
200g (approx 1½ cups) of vegan cheese
2 garlic cloves - peeled
6 tbsp of cornflour
100g (approx 1 cup) of chickpea flour
1 tsp of dried oregano
1 tsp of dried thyme
1 tsp of (gluten-free) baking powder
2 tbsp of nutritional yeast
2 tsp of paprika
Salt and pepper to taste
Olive oil

1. Add the potatoes to a large saucepan. Cover with boiling water and then simmer for 20 minutes until soft.
2. In a small bowl mix the chickpea flour, cornflour, oregano, thyme, baking powder, nutritional yeast, paprika, and salt and pepper and set aside.
3. Reserve 4 tbsp (approx ¼ cup) of the potato cooking liquid and then drain the potatoes.
4. Place the potatoes, 1 tbsp of cooking liquid, and garlic in a food processor and blend until thick and creamy. Add more cooking liquid if required.
5. Add the dry flour mix to the potatoes and blend until it becomes a doughy consistency.
6. Line two baking trays with baking paper. Place half the dough on one baking sheet and flatten it out into a circular shape about 1cm thick (wet hands if necessary). Repeat for the second pizza.
7. Bake in a preheated oven at 220°C for 10 to 12 minutes until the crust is golden and it's firm.
8. Remove pizzas and spread over the easy peasy spinach pesto, then top with sliced tomato and cheese and bake for a further 5 to 8 minutes. Serve hot or cold.

Makes 2 medium-sized pizzas

OVEN-BAKED PASTA

This is a popular Turkish staple that's like a version of lasagne, but not as saucy. Traditionally, this recipe is usually made with long strands of macaroni that look like big, fat spaghetti, but I've used penne pasta for this one.

200g (approx 2 cups) of (gluten-free) pasta
300g (approx 2 cups) of (gluten-free) soya mince or cauliflower mince (see recipe in Light Bites & Main meals)
1 onion - diced finely
1 tsp of dried mint
2 cloves of garlic - crushed and chopped
2 tbsp of flat-leaf parsley - chopped
200g (approx 1½ cups) of vegan cheese - grated
Salt and pepper to taste (this works really well with a lot of black pepper)
Olive oil for frying

For the white sauce
1 pint of soya (or almond) milk
2 tbsp of cornflour
3 tbsp of vegan butter

1. Cook the pasta according to the packet instructions. Drain and place in a deep oven dish.
2. Fry the onion in olive oil until soft and golden and add the vegan mince. Fry until it turns brown, then add to the pasta. Add salt and pepper, garlic, mint, and parsley and mix well. Then press down flat in the dish.
3. Add the sauce ingredients to a saucepan. On a medium heat whisk constantly until it boils and begins to thicken. When the sauce is a custard consistency pour over the top of the pasta and smooth down with a spatula.
4. Sprinkle the cheese on top and add a drizzle of olive oil. Cook at 180°C for 30 minutes until brown on top.

Serves 2-4

SHEPHERD'S PIE

In my pre-vegan days good, old-fashioned British shepherd's pie was a favourite of mine, and this plant-powered version is as authentic as the original. You could also top it with sweet potato for a variation.

300g (approx 2 cups) of cauliflower mince (see recipe in Light Bites & Main Meals)
4 medium potatoes – sliced finely
2 garlic cloves – crushed and chopped
1 large carrot – diced
1 leek – diced
1 courgette (zucchini) – grated coarsely
1 onion – diced
½ tsp of dried thyme
2 tsp of dried oregano
1 tsp of paprika
1 tsp of tomato puree
1 tsp of (gluten-free) soya sauce or tamari
¾ pint (approx 1½ cups) of boiling water with a (gluten-free) vegetable stock cube
100g (approx 1 cup) of frozen peas
Salt and pepper to taste
Olive oil

1. For the potatoes, place them in a large saucepan and add boiling water. Simmer on a low heat for 15 to 20 minutes until the potatoes are soft.
2. In the meantime, fry the onion in olive oil in a saucepan for 5 minutes until soft and golden. Add the rest of the ingredients and bring to the boil. Simmer for 20 minutes, adding a little more water if the sauce becomes too thick.
3. Drain the potatoes and mash them.
4. Transfer the sauce to a baking dish and press down. Spoon the mash on top, flatten, and score it into criss-cross patterns with a fork. Brush the top with olive oil and bake in a preheated oven at 180°C for 25 to 30 minutes.

Serves 4

BAKED ORANGE TOFU

I love the citrus tang that permeates this easy recipe. It's fab as a light lunch, but you could also serve it up with potato cakes (see recipe in Sides & Sundries). Any leftovers also work well added to salads or wraps.

500g block of firm tofu – drained and pressed and cut into slices about 1 cm thick
Olive oil

For the sauce
Juice and zest from 1 orange
1½ tbsp of (gluten-free) soya sauce or tamari
½ tsp of paprika
¼ tsp of chipotle chilli flakes
¼ tsp of dried oregano
1 garlic clove – pressed and chopped
1 tbsp of olive oil
Salt and pepper to taste

1. Mix all the sauce ingredients in a jug. Then place the sliced tofu in a shallow baking dish, evenly spaced out. Pour the sauce on top and marinate in the fridge for between 30 minutes and 4 hours. Afterwards, pour the marinade into a small saucepan for later use and set aside.
2. Line a baking tray with baking paper and brush on a thin coating of olive oil. Arrange the tofu in planks on the paper, evenly spaced out. The tofu should still be covered with a bit of residual marinade, but if not, brush the surface with the sauce. Bake in a preheated oven at 220°C for 15 minutes.
3. Flip the tofu over, brush a little more marinade on top, and bake for a further 10 minutes, or until the edges brown and crispen up.
4. When the tofu is ready, heat through the sauce. Drizzle on top and serve with potato cakes (see recipe in Sides & Sundries).

Serves 2

SPICY BUFFALO CAULIFLOWER BITES

These crispy little bites give you an explosion of spicy awesomeness with every mouthful. I can eat a whole batch in one go, but if there are any leftovers you can also add them to Buddha bowls.

1 medium head of cauliflower – chopped into florets

For the batter
¼ pint (approx ½ cup) of soya or almond milk
½ tsp of garlic powder
½ tsp of onion powder
4 tbsp of rice flour
¼ tsp of dried oregano
3 tbsp of cornflour
½ tsp of baking powder
1 tsp of olive oil

For the hot sauce
¼ tsp of chipotle chilli flakes
1 tsp of maple syrup
1 tsp of paprika
1 tbsp of (gluten-free) sriracha sauce
½ tsp of garlic powder
1 tbsp of vegan red wine vinegar
1 tbsp of water
¼ tsp of dried oregano
¼ tsp of smoked paprika
1 tbsp of olive oil
¼ tsp of garlic powder
Salt and pepper to taste

1. Mix the hot sauce ingredients in a large bowl and set aside.
2. Mix the batter ingredients in a large bowl. Add the cauliflower florets to the batter and toss well to coat.
3. Place the cauliflower evenly spread out on a baking tray lined with baking paper and cook in a preheated oven at 200°C for 25 minutes.
4. Remove the tray from the oven and add the cauliflower to the hot sauce bowl, coating evenly. Then spread the sauce-covered cauli back onto the baking tray and cook for another 15 minutes, until the inside is tender and the outside crispy.
5. Serve with ranch-style mayonnaise (see recipe in Meze & Dips).

Serves 2

CHINESE CURRY

I love a Chinese curry, and this recipe tastes like the authentically aromatic Chinese version. It's so easy and ready in less than the time it would take you to get a takeaway. You can also replace the soya milk with soya cream or coconut cream for an extra-rich sauce.

1 tbsp of curry powder
1 tbsp of garam masala
½ tsp of ground turmeric
½ tsp of ground cumin
½ tsp of ground coriander
1 tbsp of (gluten-free) soya sauce or tamari
1 inch piece of root ginger - peeled and grated
¾ pint (approx 1½ cups) of boiling water with a (gluten-free) vegetable stock cube
1 garlic clove - pressed and chopped
¼ pint (approx ½ cup) of soya milk
3 oyster mushrooms - diced
1 carrot - in shavings or sliced finely
2 spring onions - sliced
100g (approx 1 cup) of frozen peas
2 tbsp of cornflour
Salt and pepper to taste
Sesame oil for frying

1. Mix the milk and cornflour together and set aside.
2. Fry the onion and mushrooms in sesame oil in a saucepan for a few minutes until browned.
3. Add the dried spices and stir for a few minutes. Then add the rest of the ingredients, apart from the milk and cornflour.
4. Cover and simmer for 10 minutes.
5. Add the milk/cornflour mixture and stir through until the sauce thickens. Serve with rice or rice noodles.

Serves 2

SICILIAN AUBERGINE PASTA

Based on the Sicilian classic, this is a quick but satisfying meal for pasta lovers with a full-on, intensely Italian flavour.

200g of (gluten-free) pasta
2 aubergines - sliced thinly and chopped in half
2 garlic cloves - crushed and chopped
1 onion - diced
4 large tomatoes - grated with juice
½ a red chilli
1 to 2 tbsp of fresh basil - chopped finely
Olive oil for frying
Salt and pepper to taste

Garnish
Sprinkling of quick parmesan (see recipe in Sides & Sundries)

1. Cook the pasta according to the packet instructions.
2. In the meantime, fry the onions for a few minutes. Add the chilli, garlic, tomatoes, basil, and salt and pepper. Cover and simmer on low heat for 5 minutes.
3. Fry the aubergine slices in a large frying pan in olive oil until soft and golden.
4. Drain the pasta and add back into the cooking pot. Add the aubergines and sauce and mix together well before serving.

Serves 2-4

TURKISH BEAN STEW

Filling, midweek dinners have never been so easy. This flavoursome, hearty dish will tantalize your taste buds and give you a protein hit in one go. It goes well served with vermicelli rice (see recipes in Sides & Sundries).

400g can of cannellini beans - drained and rinsed
2 garlic cloves - crushed and chopped
2 spring onions - sliced
2 large tomatoes - diced
1 large carrot - grated
1 green cubanelle pepper (or regular bell pepper) - diced
½ tsp of chilli flakes *optional*
½ pint (approx 1 cup) of boiled water with a (gluten-free) vegetable stock cube
2 tsp of paprika
Salt and pepper to taste
Olive oil for frying

Garnish
Chopped flat-leaf parsley

1. Fry the onions and pepper in a saucepan for 5 minutes until golden and soft.
2. Add the rest of the ingredients then cover and simmer for 20 minutes.
3. Garnish with parsley and serve.

Serves 2

STUFFED PEPPERS

Mediterranean people like to stuff things! You may recognize the word "dolma" as those parcels of rice stuffed into vine leaves and wrapped. But it doesn't end there. You can also stuff tomatoes, courgettes (zucchinis), aubergines, and tomatoes. I'm using bell peppers for this recipe, but you can use any of the veggies above.

Variation: You can swap the filling for my cooked Indian mushroom rice or vegetable pilaf if you prefer (see recipes in Sides & Sundries).

4 bell peppers
300g (approx 2 cups) of (gluten-free) soya mince or cauliflower mince (see recipe in Light Bites & Main Meals)
3 mushrooms - diced
2 garlic cloves - crushed and chopped
1 onion - diced
3 tbsp of flat-leaf parsley - chopped
1 tbsp of dried oregano
2 tbsp of tomato puree
1 tomato - peeled and diced
½ pint (approx 1 cup) of boiling water
Salt and pepper to taste
2 tbsp of olive oil

1. Cut the tops off the peppers but don't throw them away, as you'll need them later. Remove any seeds from inside.
2. Fry the onion in olive oil for 5 minutes until soft, then add the garlic and mushrooms. Cook for a few minutes before adding the mince. Stir for 5 minutes to cook through.
3. Add the parsley, oregano, tomato, tomato puree, salt and pepper, and mix thoroughly.
4. Spoon the mixture into the peppers, but be careful not to overfill them. Replace the lids of the peppers as tightly as possible and place them in the bottom of a baking dish that's wide enough to keep them upright.
5. Pour the boiling water around the peppers and cook in a preheated oven at 180°C for 25 to 30 minutes, until the peppers are soft.

Serves 2-4

KUNG PAO TOFU

Crispy-tender tofu combined with a sweet, sour, spicy, and peanutty taste sensation. Sound good? I hope so, because this mouthwatering meal is a delicious explosion of ecstasy and healthier than the takeaway version.

500g block of firm tofu - drained and pressed and cut into cubes
Olive oil
6 tbsp of cornflour
1 tsp of paprika
1 green pepper - diced
1 red pepper - diced
2 spring onions - diced
1 red chilli - deseeded and chopped
2 tbsp of unsalted peanuts - toasted

For the sauce
3 tbsp of maple syrup
4 tbsp of (gluten-free) soya sauce or tamari
¼ pint (approx ½ cup) of water
1 tsp of white rice vinegar
2 tsp of cornflour
2 garlic cloves - pressed and chopped
1 inch piece of root ginger - grated
1 tbsp of sesame oil
Salt and pepper to taste

Garnish
Sesame seeds

1. Mix the sauce ingredients and set aside.
2. For the tofu, mix the cornflour and paprika in a bowl. Add the drained tofu and toss until it's evenly coated.
3. Line a baking tray with baking paper and brush on a thin coating of olive oil. Add the tofu, making sure it's evenly spaced out. Bake in a preheated oven at 220°C for 15 minutes, then stir the tofu around to make sure it's cooking evenly and bake for another 15 minutes until it's golden and crispy
4. In the meantime, fry the onion, peppers, and chilli in the sesame oil until soft. Add the peanuts and the jug of sauce, and stir on a medium heat until it thickens up. Pour on top of the baked tofu, sprinkle with sesame seeds, and serve with rice or noodles.

Serves 2

CREAMY STROGANOFF

Feel free to swap the oyster mushrooms for any shrooms of your choice. This has a really rich, creamy taste, but if you don't have soya cream you can replace that with 200g of silken tofu blitzed in a blender until smooth or ½ pint (approx 1 cup) of plant-based milk mixed with 1 tbsp of cornflour.

5 large oyster mushrooms - sliced
2 garlic cloves - pressed and chopped
1 green pepper - sliced
1 red onion - sliced
Juice of half a lemon
1 tsp of tomato puree
4 tbsp of soya cream
2 tsp of paprika
¼ tsp of smoked paprika
3 tbsp of flat-leaf parsley - chopped
25g (approx ½ cup) of frozen green beans
*optional
½ pint (approx 1 cup) of boiling water with a (gluten-free) vegetable stock cube
Salt to taste
Olive oil for frying

1. In a jug mix the stock, tomato puree, and lemon juice, then set aside.
2. In a saucepan fry the pepper and onion in olive oil for a few minutes. Add the mushrooms and fry for a couple of minutes until browned.
3. Add the rest of the ingredients, except for the soya cream and parsley, then simmer for 10 minutes.
4. Stir in the soya cream and parsley to heat through. Serve with rice or roast potatoes.

Serves 2

MARINADES

Here are a few more marinade suggestions that you can use for tofu dishes, roasted veggies, cauliflower steaks, veggie kebabs, or (if you're not following a gluten-free diet) tempeh and seitan. All you need to do is find your weapon of choice, mix the ingredients in a shallow dish, and marinate to death!

Lemon and Paprika
Juice and zest of ½ a lemon
1 tbsp of olive oil
½ tsp of paprika
¼ tsp of chilli flakes
¼ tsp of lemon thyme
Salt and pepper to taste

Yoghurt Tikka
4 tbsp of vegan yoghurt
¼ tsp of ground cumin
¼ tsp of ground turmeric
¼ tsp of paprika
¼ tsp of ground coriander
1 tbsp of olive oil
Salt and pepper to taste

Satay Sauce
1 tsp of sesame oil
4 tbsp of crunchy peanut butter
1 tbsp of (gluten-free) soya sauce or tamari
1 tbsp of maple syrup
¼ tsp of chilli flakes
1 garlic clove - crushed and chopped

Ginger and Lime
½ inch piece of root ginger - peeled and grated
1 tbsp of lime juice
1 tbsp of olive oil
1 tbsp of maple syrup
½ tsp of sriracha sauce

Sesame and Soya Sauce
1 tbsp of (gluten-free) soya sauce or tamari
1 tbsp of maple syrup
1 tsp of sesame oil
1 garlic clove - crushed and chopped
1 tsp of sesame seeds
Salt and pepper to taste

Spicy Pineapple and Chilli
2 tbsp of pineapple juice
½ a chilli - deseeded and chopped finely
1 tbsp of olive oil
1 tbsp of maple syrup
Sprinkling of ground black pepper
Salt to taste

About the Author

Sibel Hodge is the author of the No 1 fiction Bestsellers Look Behind You, Untouchable, Duplicity, Into the Darkness, and Their Last Breath. Her books have sold over one million copies and are international bestsellers in the UK, USA, Australia, France, Canada and Germany. She writes in an eclectic mix of genres, and is a passionate human and animal rights advocate.

Her work has been nominated and shortlisted for numerous prizes, including the Harry Bowling Prize, the Yeovil Literary Prize, the Chapter One Promotions Novel Competition, The Romance Reviews' prize for Best Novel with Romantic Elements and Indie Book Bargains' Best Indie Book of 2012 in two categories. She was the winner of Best Children's Book in the 2013 eFestival of Words; nominated for the 2015 BigAl's Books and Pals Young Adult Readers' Choice Award; winner of the Crime, Thrillers & Mystery Book from a Series Award in the SpaSpa Book Awards 2013; winner of the Readers' Favorite Young Adult (Coming of Age) Honorable award in 2015; a New Adult finalist in the Oklahoma Romance Writers of America's International Digital Awards 2015, 2017 International Thriller Writers Award finalist for Best E-book Original Novel, Honorable Mention Award Winner in the USA 2018 Reader's Choice Awards, and winner of the No 1 Best Thriller in the Top Shelf Magazine Indie Book Awards 2018! Her novella Trafficked: The Diary of a Sex Slave has been listed as one of the top forty books about human rights by Accredited Online Colleges.

For Sibel's latest book releases, giveaways and gossip, sign up to her newsletter at: www.sibelhodge.com

Also by Sibel Hodge

Non-Fiction

Deliciously Vegan Soup Kitchen
Healing Meditations for Surviving Grief and Loss

Fiction

Dark Shadows
Their Last Breath
The Disappeared
Into the Darkness
Beneath the Surface
Duplicity
Untouchable
Where the Memories Lie
Look Behind You
Butterfly
Trafficked: The Diary of a Sex Slave
Fashion, Lies, and Murder (Amber Fox Mystery No 1)
Money, Lies, and Murder (Amber Fox Mystery No 2)
Voodoo, Lies, and Murder (Amber Fox Mystery No 3)
Chocolate, Lies, and Murder (Amber Fox Mystery No 4)
Santa Claus, Lies, and Murder (Amber Fox Mystery No 4.5)
Vegas, Lies, and Murder (Amber Fox Mystery No 5)
Murder and Mai Tais (Danger Cove Cocktail Mystery No 1)
Killer Colada (Danger Cove Cocktail Mystery No 2)
The See-Through Leopard
Fourteen Days Later
My Perfect Wedding
The Baby Trap
It's a Catastrophe

Printed in Great Britain
by Amazon